Flying High with Literacy 2

Uni

Sub

Also avaliable from The Questions Publishing Company Ltd:

Flying High with Literacy 1
Quality teaching in literacy

Joy McCormick and Narinderjit Gill
ISBN: 1-84190-017-6

Flying High with Literacy 2

Quality learning through a range of genres

Joy McCormick and Narinderjit Gill

The Questions Publishing Company Ltd
Birmingham
1999

First published in 1999
by The Questions Publishing Company Ltd
27 Frederick Street, Birmingham B1 3HH

Designed by Al Stewart
Cover design by Lisa Martin
Illustrations by Martin Cater

ISBN: 1-84190-018-4

Contents

Acknowledgements

Our initial thanks must go to Mick Waters who motivated and inspired us to share and celebrate our work in classrooms. The practical examples on which this book is based could not have been carried out without the support of children and teachers in Sandwell LEA who were involved in the Quality Start Raising Standards Project.

We would also like to extend our thanks to:

▲ Grove Vale Primary and Leasowes Primary for providing us with children's work.
▲ Janice Wrigley who worked alongside teachers and developed the work at Grove Vale Primary.
▲ Wendy Bloom for her insightful advice on catering for children with Special Educational Needs.
▲ Jan Roman for her support during the final stages of publication.

And last, but not least, warm thanks to our families for their patience and support during all the long evenings, weekends and holidays that we spent working on the materials.

The photograph of Indian women at a water pump (page 6) appears by courtesy of TRIP/H Rogers. The photograph of a child turning on a bath tap (page 6) appears by courtesy of John Birdsall Photography. 'One Evening in the Bay of

Foreword

The Quality Start – Raising Standards in Primary Schools – project has been one of the major contributors to raising achievement and improving the quality of teaching in Sandwell primary schools. The project, which provides in-service training, follow-up classroom support and resources, has enabled teachers to enhance pupils' learning of basic skills and to develop their own teaching methodology.

Improvements in teacher morale and motivation, in pupil response and achievement are evident across the borough. The project has also facilitated the celebration and sharing of good practice between schools and has demonstrated that there is a wealth of talent in Sandwell. The LEA was inspected in 1998 and Quality Start was highlighted for its significant impact on the quality of teaching.

Through the work of the project a range of teacher support materials have been developed by project staff in partnership with schools. These form the basis of this series of publications, and are a testimony to the talented leaders in Sandwell schools. The project has been developed in partnership with the St Martin's College, Lancaster, and we thank them for their contribution to ensuring that our young children receive a quality start.

Stuart Gallacher
Chief Education Officer, Sandwell

Preface

Flying High with Literacy 1 and 2 stem from work developed during an innovative school improvement project which began in Sandwell LEA in the West Midlands in 1996 and will finish in April 2000. 'Quality Start' has involved all of the primary schools in the LEA, with teachers considering the quality of their own teaching and collaborating in pairs to plan and develop the ways they work with children. Inservice sessions and the support of seconded teachers to work alongside them in classrooms have enabled different teachers to develop their own practice and critically review strengths and areas for further development. Support from headteachers has resulted in ideas being adopted across the school in many instances and the production of whole school 'teaching and learning' policies.

Quality Start has been an exciting project, and throughout its five years has had to adapt to different educational and political initiatives. The most important of these has been the National Literacy Strategy, with its emphasis on both the content of the reading/writing curriculum and the ways in which this content should be taught. These books focus on the teaching of literacy and will enable teachers to consider different ways of working (the practical ideas we all need) but also the rationale which underpins the ideas (why these ideas are so powerful). Book One examines the notion of high quality teaching and learning in the literacy hour. Any element of the hour can be approached in different ways, and indeed this variation will be vital as children build up a history of hundreds of such hours – the excitement being reported in many classrooms currently could easily turn into a classroom ritual – and then the thinking will stop. So, for example, there are many ways of teaching plenaries which will create the conditions necessary for children to consider critically what they have achieved and what they have learnt. Book Two focuses on the teaching of writing, with its emphasis on the range of text types outlined in the National

Literacy Strategy. Again a tremendous number of ideas are included, each of which can be developed in many different ways. Each book stands alone but they complement each other so that together there is advice and ideas for teaching which come to us directly from primary classrooms.

Joy and Narinder have been key figures in the development and success of Quality Start. Their creativity in considering classroom issues and developing practical ways of addressing them has been one of the features of the project. These two books contain the results of this work and primary teachers will find them extremely useful as they look to develop the ways in which they teach.

Tony Martin
The Educational Development Unit
St. Martin's College, Lancaster

Introduction: working with different genres

This book has emerged from the work done with children and teachers in classrooms on the Quality Start Project, in Sandwell in the West Midlands. Aimed at raising the achievement of children, the project explored techniques and strategies that enhanced teaching and learning and provoked teachers into thinking about why they teach the way they do.

Children need to be introduced to, allowed to explore and interact with different genres before they can produce their own pieces of non-fiction. A common problem that we found while working with teachers on the project was that it was often very difficult for them to locate suitable text to use. As a result pieces of text had to be created that did provide appropriate scaffolds to support the writers in developing their own 'copy'.

The materials we have subsequently developed provide teachers with a source of ideas that have been trialled in the classroom to help build children's literacy skills, and have been proven to raise children's achievement. All the pieces of text provided will not be found in any literature and have been written with a purpose in mind, although the photocopiable materials may be used in a variety of ways.

Each section tackles a different genre of writing and can stand as a unit of study either with the whole class or for group activities. Each section also has a pattern, beginning with an approach to studying a piece of text, then giving examples of class/group activities and a framework to support writing a piece of text, then finally offering ideas for where the writing can be used afterwards, i.e. a purpose for producing it. Extracts of planning and practice have been used to enable teachers to interpret ideas more easily and instantly into their own classrooms, and can be used as they stand, or as a starting point to leap off from and fly with!

Writing frames

Before we begin with the genre-specific sections, here are a few pointers about using writing frames effectively. Writing frames provide a skeleton outline for a piece of writing around which children structure their own ideas.

Key things to bear in mind when using writing frames:

▲ Model and discuss how to use the frame first, before jointly completing one. In their book *Writing Across the Curriculum* (Reading and Language Information Centre, 1998), Lewis and Wray provide examples of a range of writing frames that can be used, and refer to this stage as 'joint construction' between teacher and child/group. After the modelling stage, the child should be ready to undertake writing supported by the frame. The examples that follow in this book show these frames being used at different stages.

▲ Remember that not all the children in a class will need to use a writing frame. It should only be introduced if a child needs extra support for his or her writing. It is also important to be clear about the purpose for the child to be writing – the frame itself should never be seen as a purpose for writing.

▲ Children need to be taught to view the frame as part of the drafting process in writing and therefore they can cross out, amend and add to the frame accordingly.

▲ Writing frames can provide a structure for texts and raise awareness with children about generic structures. However, we need to be careful not to use writing frames to teach children about generic structures as this could leave them with the message that they are rigid and unchangeable. Frames are only a small part of the varied and rich writing experiences we offer children.

1
Report writing

Lesson Plan

Whole Class Work – Text Study (see text on page 3)
Look at the title of the passage – what do the class think the passage will be about?
Introduce it as a piece of report writing.
Whole class shared read of the passage 'Life in the country'.
Ask what part of the world they think it was written about.
Can they justify this by reference to the text?

Get children into the text further by reading each paragraph in turn and encouraging children to do a word hunt, e.g. skimming for and underlining/highlighting words or phrases which tell us facts about:

a) materials used;
b) something they don't have.

At the end ask if they have discovered something which would be a really important thing to have if you lived in the country.

Class/Group Activities
1. Homes in India – using a comparison grid to develop note-taking skills (see pages 6 and 7).
2. Writing a report – looking at the sentence structures within report writing and encouraging children to write in the same way (see page 8).
3. Choosing a home – sorting information from passage into list form and developing evaluative comprehension (see page 9).
4. Looking for adjectives – word study (see page 10).
5. Team challenge – question raising, could also be used to

support thinking about the main idea contained within each paragraph (see page 11).

Plenary
Possible feedback:

1. How many differences did you find? Which place would you rather live in – city or country?
2. Read out children's writing – ask the class to comment upon whether the ideas were presented well. Start to collect examples of 1-, 2- and 3-word phrases for class lists.
3. Discuss the answers to some of the questions asked at the bottom of the worksheet.
4. Collect lists of adjectives beginning with the letter '____'; set spelling challenges for some of the words, using the 'look, cover, write, check' approach.
5. Ask groups to challenge each other group with one of the questions raised, and see how long it takes for them to come up with the answer.

Follow-up Work

Children could present their information in a travellers' guide to India – children who have recently travelled to the country could also add any photographs they might have. The guide could then be produced for inclusion in the school library and/ or part of resources for use in other classes.

Life in the country

Houses in the country are often made of stone with tiled roofs. This keeps the rain out but the rooms are small and overcrowded. Some have large areas of land around them which are used for farming. The windows are usually open with no shutters or screens fitted to keep out any mosquitoes. Instead, a coil burns throughout the night and sets off an incense-like smell which keeps the insects away. Sometimes mosquito nets are used over the beds to keep the insects out too.

Usually there are no toilets inside the houses and people have to squat in the fields, by the river or use a bucket instead. There is also little electricity or running water. All water has to be boiled after being collected from deep wells.

Not all villages have televisions, but where there is one everyone in the village gathers around to watch it.

Inside the houses there are no private bedrooms and everyone sleeps on their own mat on the floor, or on a woven string bed out in the courtyard under the stars. There is no separate dining room and people sit on the mud floor of the kitchen with a brass or steel plate, or even a leaf to eat from. Sometimes in the evening the meal is served outside with the men sitting on string cots away from the women. A lot of the time fingers are used to eat with rather than a knife and fork.

In some of the mud huts where people live the walls are covered in cow-dung paste and painted with wonderful designs. However, in the very hot weather the housing materials begin to suffer - mud crumbles and wood swells – people find that doors and windows suddenly won't close.

Life in the city

Millions of people live in the cities of India. It seems sometimes that every space is filled, and wherever you look human beings are to be found in between the 'shipwrecked' features of old, derelict buildings. The busiest parts of the town are filled with people from the villages, hoping for a better life in the city. As many as five people find shelter under a thatched construction leaning against an old stone wall of a house. Others live on the roadside under make-shift shelters of wood, cardboard, tins and pieces of cloth. Inside there are a few boxes in one room which measures 3 metres by 4 metres. Everything happens in these squats - people live and die, eat and sleep, buy and sell. If you haven't got something you invent it or use your imagination to build it.

In other parts of the city there are concrete blocks of flats called colonies. Here it seems as if some homes were built and then someone came along and built more in between them. Inside each flat is a large living room where all the family eat together around a large table laid with tablecloth, napkins and cutlery. There is no private bedroom and the bedding can be rolled out whenever it is needed. There is also a bathroom with a toilet.

In the bigger cities big houses may be found with beautiful gardens surrounded by high walls. Marble floors can be mopped in the afternoon, and the windows and curtains closed to keep the inside of the house cool. Air conditioning may also be used. These houses are highly protected with prison-like bars at the windows and heavy padlocks at the doors. A local watchman guards at night and warns off thieves with a whistle and by banging a big stick. This can keep the owners awake.

Not every house has a telephone and sometimes people can wait years to have one put in. Even then, when the monsoon season begins the lines break down and you need to pay someone to keep the line in order.

Fresh water is also a problem and the poor have to queue up in the streets to get it. Others may have their own personal water tanks attached to their houses, but these need to be scrubbed clean or the water turns brown as it traps the dirt. At certain times there is no water supply and water has to be stored. Electricity too can be suddenly cut off and any air conditioning stops. Life then can be very hot and uncomfortable for everyone. Windows cannot be left open either if the local pest control is spraying chemicals into the air to kill any mosquitoes.

Homes in India

Look at the two photographs below, then tell a partner what you notice about them. In what ways are they different?

Consider some of the differences that you might expect to find between houses found in the country and houses found in the city. Record your thoughts like a list using the grid provided – one idea has been written in to start you off.

Use your passage to help find out if you were correct. Underline any key words which show the differences. Make some notes about the differences in the boxes.

Comparison grid – homes in India

Differences	Houses in the city	Houses in the country
Water supply	Personal water tanks	Collected from deep wells

Writing a report: sentence beginnings

As you were reading your passage you should have noticed some special ways of starting off a sentence.

In other parts . . .   .

Not every . . .   .

Inside . . .   .

Can you find and record other examples using 1, 2 and 3 words?

Now have a go at reporting how *you* live in the city/country using some of these sentence starts in your writing.

Choosing a home

If you were going to live in a city in India, there would be different types of homes where you might live. Think of the things an estate agent might say to try to persuade you to have each of these homes.

Questions to think about:

What do you think is valued most by people living in each house?

How would it feel to live in each of these houses?

How do they compare with what you would say about your own home in the UK?

Discuss your answers with the rest of your group or class.

Looking for adjectives

How many adjectives can you think of to describe Indian houses in . . .

The city?

H

O

M

E

S

The country?

H

O

M

E

S

Team challenge

Read your passage again with a partner and at the end of each paragraph think of a question that you could find an answer to.

Write your questions below.

Now give your questions to another team and see if they can answer them!

(The team with the most answers wins.)

2
Report writing – newspaper reports

Lesson Plan

Whole Class Work – Text Study
Children need to work with a sample newspaper report to get the structure of report writing. Use the worksheet 'Being a reporter' on page 14 to:

a)   analyse the types of questions reporters ask;
b)   find the answers from the article.

Class/Group Activities
Read a section of a story which has an 'incident' in it. Using role play, explore the characters in the scene and think of some expressions or actions which would represent some of them. Recreate the scene in frames. Ask the children to decide which parts of the text go into each frame.

Combine all the frames into one 'snapshot'. Let one half of the class take their places in the snapshot while others try to guess who the individual characters are by their frozen actions. What kind of statement would the others have said about the incident to their friends?

One group of children could plan how they would respond in role to the questions posed by a newspaper reporter covering the story. The rest of the class could then be the reporters and use the previous prompt sheet 'Being a reporter' to think of some suitable questions to ask.

Plenary
Teacher-led question and answer session with group of characters.

Follow-up work

Using the responses the children could work in pairs to produce a front page spread. Explore the arts of editing and proof reading. A picture could then be added using the original story as stimulus, or provided by a polaroid picture of the group dressed as the characters frozen in action.

Further ideas

In order to explore newspapers successfully we need to consider certain criteria when selecting appropriate examples to use. Children could also use this list of criteria in response to what they read. An example of a review sheet that they might use is shown on page 15. Newspaper work need not be done in isolation from other genres. For example, following a shared reading session using a piece of poetry about fishing, there may be thematic links to general interest magazines, e.g. *Anglers' Weekly*. The case study that follows (see page 16) shows how you might plan to use this link during the literacy hour and in supporting group activities.

Useful resources

For further help on how to use newspapers in education, look up the Northcliffe Newspaper Group's website, which contains lots of useful resources to send for. Their website address is: **http://www.nie.northcliffe.co.uk/index.html**
They also have details of how to get copies of an activity newspaper sent directly to your school. There are six editions per year with a range of non-fiction texts. Each edition is accompanied by reference to certain elements of the literacy framework for that term.

Some important questions to ask:

Who?	What?	Why?
Where?	When?	How?

Being a reporter – getting the story

Who was involved?	What happened?
Why is it newsworthy?	Where did the story happen?
When did the event occur?	How did it happen?
Any other information?	

Newspapers checklist –
taking a closer look

Headlines

Are they eye-catching? What makes them so?
Do they make you want to find out more and read on?
Can you find any that use homonyms?
What are the key words that fit with the story behind a report?

Photographs

Do they help you understand what has been written?
What are the 'qualities' that make a picture interesting? Look at a few pictures to find out.

Text

How easy is it to read and understand? What makes it so?
Can you find any words that you are unsure about – how might you try to work out what they mean?
Would you be able to write about similar experiences or events?
Could you find the answers to questions starting with how?, what?, when?, why? or where? after reading one of the reports?

Layout

What are the good points and bad points about trying to locate information in the newspaper?
How does the layout help the reader to find their way around?

Case Study: NLP Literacy Hour Plan

Whole class work: shared reading and word study work with the poem *One evening in the Bay of Lipari . . .* by Michael Rosen (see pages 18–21).

Orientate the children to the poem: no rhyme, author's name, untitled. Ask them to scan the opening section and see if they can guess what it is about.

Section 1: (page 18)
What is the poem about?
What kinds of things is the fisherman using? Find and underline the key words that describe the rod, the line, the float, the hook and the bread.
What do they think a 'rainbow' fish looks like?
Predict what the fisherman is going to do with the fish when he has caught them.

Section 2: (page 19)
Choose from:
- ▲ look at the phrase 'five middling . . .' and play about with the order of this repeated phrase';
- ▲ explore the jumbled phrases of the second verse, reflecting the movement of the eel;
- ▲ look for repeated phrases which order events in the third verse.

Did the fisherman get the eel? What happened?

Section 3: (page 20)
Has the number of the fish changed in this section?
Look at the description about catching a fish. Can the children recall a time when they have caught a fish too? Are there similarities with their experiences? What else might the poet have mentioned?

Section 4: (page 21)
How do the children feel about the fish that has been caught?
How would the class like the poem to end? Do they want the fish to live?

Final thoughts

How does the poem make the children feel about fishing?
The poem has no title. What might the title be if they could
give it one?

Follow-up activities

1 Ask the children to read through the short fishing report
   from *Anglers' Mail* magazine (see page 22). Using the
   grid, get them to collect information and identify the
   main features of the report, i.e. name of angler, job,
   place, type and size of fish caught, time of day, type of
   bait used, further comments.
   Writing extension: children could produce their own
   written report on their own catch, using the grid to
   collect information first.

2 Reproduce a page of *Anglers' Mail* advertising fishing
   holidays abroad. Ask the children to find out what kinds
   of information is needed to write the advertising copy.
   Then they can design their own advert using information
   collected from the poem read as a class. For example:
   where? Bay of Lipari, Spain; accommodation? hotel
   overlooking the harbour; who with? organised by the
   fisherman; further comments? harbour fishing, telephone
   number, etc.

3 Ask the children to collect words associated with fishing.
   They can then find underlined words in the poem and
   illustrate them. Ask them to supply further ideas of their
   own (especially when considering the type of bait
   needed). Try designing a poster entitled 'Things to take
   when fishing'.

One evening in the Bay of Lipari . . .
by Michael Rosen

One evening in the bay of Lipari
on rocks that look over the harbour water
a man sits with his chin stuck into his shoulder
fishing for rainbow fish
with a long green rod and line.

Crouching in the pools behind him
we collect the rainbows in a beer crate
watching on that line.
The float dips. The man doesn't move.
We flick the water across the fish to keep
them fresh,
the sun stands still against the tower
and its shadow falls across the water.

Then the rod whips, up flies the float –
but nothing more. Thirteen rainbows it stays.
We watch him roll a roll of bread in his mouth
to bait his hook again
and we duck
as past our ears go bread hook and float
all on the end of the long rod and line.

Thirteen rainbows out of the sea.
It can't be bad. Fourteen would be better.
More fish; more soup. There's five middling,
five tiddlers and three whoppers.
Or if you stack them up the other way
three whoppers, five middling, five tiddlers.
We have a line too, because under these rocks
live moray eels.

Yards and yards of eel, writhing about
just where the round the edge
where the over the through the under
where there here, where we lower our hook
with a lump of raw rainbow dangling.

No sooner said
when yes he'd slid out
and taken the bait. He's got it.
We've got it. He takes the bait.
he takes the hook. He takes the hook
he takes the line – he'll have your fingers too.

Let go pull him
he pulls, pull him, I said. The line breaks,
and without a turn about or round about
he's in reverse and slides back along his tracks
to where it is his tracks backtrack to.

The sun sets behind the tower.
Three whoppers, five middling and five or
four or five... Four tiddlers –
Can't be bad.

The man's float still rises and falls.
He knows there's more where they came
from.
He can feel them nibbling down there.
You can almost see them cruising
in a complete quiet
in the last rays of the day
the line dropping out of the light above
down to where the nudge about very cool
gliding round this right little chunk
of sweet nibble lump thing
that breaks off crumbs in the current
if you can bear to wait
if they can wait.

We wait.
One can't.
The whole lump he takes. The lot.
And up, up out of the quiet
into the sky like a silver bird
wey op wey op wey op
he's on the line
his last moment is a ride in the sky
wild, he flies on air with his fins
he must fall
and down he swings
once fast past the man's hand
once slap into it.
He holds that fish's wriggle alright
and takes his hook back
flings it to us on the rocks.

There's still life.
There's still heart and blood
the fins still stretch for the water.
He flips so strong
it could carry him to Spain and back –
underwater.
Here it turns him over and over
somersaulter
he keeps flipping.
Perhaps he can feel the smell of water
only inches away.
He keeps flipping for that water.
He could make it.
If we didn't like fish soup
he could really make it.
We're on to him,
get our fingers round his belly
slide them down to that flashy tail
and crack his head against the rock.

Crack it again number fourteen
crack it once more and put him down.
Lie him down in the old beer crate.
He's middling.
Three whoppers, four tiddlers, six middlers.
Thirteen. Thirteen? I thought –
The old thirteen is being minced with line and hook
in a cold black crack by the moray eel
in the rocks somewhere.
Time for us to go.

As we leave, climbing over the rocks
back to the road,
the man looks out across the harbour
and near across a rubbish tip
where all the pots bottles boxes and crates in
the world
have come.
He looks up the cliff above the tip
to the hotel that empties and drops the pots
and spits.

We'll have soup
so long as we've got fish
Come on.

Fishing report

Name _____

Job _____

Address _____

Place _____

Time of day _____

Fish caught _____

Bait _____

Other comments _____

_____

_____

Jim Jones had a good start to his day trip to the River Severn. He managed to net 20lb of chub in the first few hours. Jim, a lorry driver from the Midlands, used spicy maggots with a 3lb line and size 16 hook. He was really pleased and the sun shone all day!

3
Discussion

Lesson Plan

Whole Class Work – Text Study

Shared read of discussion paper (see page 25). Following this, model how to highlight the text which shows arguments for and arguments against (using two colours). Children then continue the process with a partner.

Focus on word level work: give the children the challenge of underlining a special phrase which has been used to 'frame' the argument. Talk through examples of special vocabulary. Let the children continue to search for five minutes. Then brainstorm the characteristics of the genre:

- ▲ sequence of statements, i.e. opening, arguments and elaboration, reiteration of key points and summary;
- ▲ use of vocabulary;
- ▲ factual evidence, no 'bias';
- ▲ appeals to emotions but not 'emotive';
- ▲ demonstrates point of view.

Class/Group Activities

Provide children with a controversial statement for discussion/ debate, e.g. 'Children should do homework every day'.

Split children into groups of three, and explain that each person within the group has a role to play: pupil, teacher, parent. Give 'role cards' out for them to hold. Children need to remember that what they will say in the group will be the words or statements that a pupil, teacher or parent might use. They must also use examples or evidence to support their arguments that are based on fact.

Provide each group with an enlarged discussion grid on which to record arguments for and arguments against the statement (see page 27 for an example). Appoint a group scribe. After ten minutes ask the children to come to a conclusion in their groups by weighing up all the different points of view.

Children can then consider the key phrases/words used within the discussion grid and use these to put together a verbal report. A collaborative piece of writing may be set out in the space at the bottom of the grid.

Plenary
Ask one group to read out what they felt to be their conclusion. Other groups can debate whether they agree or not by reference to their discussion grids. Encourage the use of special vocabulary within the debate.

Follow-up Work
Writing a discussion paper can also be a natural extension of other debates which take place in the classroom.

After forming a point of view, children can then be encouraged to look at persuasive writing. Again this can involve some study at word and sentence level to determine key features and layout of this genre, which is not too dissimilar to a discussion paper. This may lead to children writing their points of view coherently for submission to a school council, or for use in the production of leaflets for distribution both inside and outside school.

The situation I am facing is whether to go on holiday with my parents this year or spend the time at camp instead. My friends think it would be cool to be allowed to go away on your own but my parents are worried about me looking after myself for the first time.

Some people say that camp is really enjoyable. Everyone stays up till late. You get to make your own decisions instead of your parents telling you what to do all the time. They say it's good to learn to do things on your own.
This year people say it will be really special because we will be going on a boat trip for one of the days.
All the people who have been to camp have enjoyed having lots of different things to do each day. They have a great laugh when they play tricks on each other.

On the other hand my parents think that some people who go to camp are not to be trusted. Somebody had to come home last year because they had all their sleeping kit ruined. My mum says that I'll lose things because I always have to be reminded to put things away safely.
A lot of my friends have said they aren't going this year because they get sea sick. The idea that they will have to do jobs around the camp every day also makes it sound tiring.
My sister likes to go away with our parents because when her pocket money runs out, they always give her some more to spend. The best thing is that they will all be going to stay in a big hotel near the sea this year.

My opinion is that it might be best for me to wait another year because more of my friends may go then. I could also save up for all the trips and I will be a lot older and more experienced. Therefore, I have decided to go on holiday with my parents this year.

Role cards

pupil

teacher

parent

Discussion grid

Some people say / The idea that / Furthermore / The most important point is	Arguments for (advantages)	On the other hand / However / They argue that / Some might disagree	Arguments against (disadvantages)

Conclusion

4

Giving instructions: recipes

Lesson Plan

Whole Class Work – Text Study

Give each group a selection of recipes.

Explain to the children that you want them to look at the samples of 'writing' that they have in front of them. Can they work out what kind of writing we are going to focus upon for the lesson? Give them one minute to scan the writing.

Ask the question: 'Why did you think they were all recipes?' What were the main features that they identified? Explain that we are looking at how the recipe has been set out – the layout. Ask the children to work in pairs and talk for 2 minutes about how the writing has been set out. Brainstorm some ideas as a class and then ask the children to make a list of as many features as they can find. Model how to make a list to avoid children using lengthy sentences.

After three minutes get the children to swap partners and encourage them to tell a partner what they found out. With their new partners they can think about how each of the features helps the reader. Brainstorm these ideas as a whole class – ask one person to call out the feature while the other says how it helps the reader.

Features of recipe books:

Contents	Instructional diagrams
Introduction	Abbreviations
Glossary	Conversion charts
Lists	Headings
Numbered instructions	Subheadings

Word level work (Verbs and prepositions)

Consider how the text has been written. Is it asking, persuading or telling the reader to do something? What kinds of things is it telling us to do?

Can the children work with a partner and underline some of the verbs which tell us to do something? Where do we find them? Teaching point: using the verb at the start of the sentence brings more emphasis to the word. Give two examples of where the verb is used in different places, e.g. 'You need to get a piece of paper.' 'Get a piece of paper.' What difference do the children find? (It becomes more of an order.)

Write a phrase on the board with a verb and a preposition – 'Roll out'. What has happened here? Get the children to talk about the difference between 'Roll the pastry' and 'Roll out the pastry'. Make the teaching point that prepositions make the instructions clearer. Ask the children to search for any other combinations of prepositions and verbs. Begin to make a class list of those found after two minutes.

Other word/sentence level features

Adverbs	Abbreviations	Use of parentheses/ brackets for further explanation
Use of colon	Synonyms	Statements – explanations/definitions
Repetitive use of comma		

Class/Group Activities

Ask the children to think about a recipe as a set of instructions of how to prepare and do something (in this case 'make' something). Explain that instructions aren't always about making things. However, written instructions, whatever they are for, can behave in the same way, i.e. they still have headings, lists of what you need, a sequence of tasks, and diagrams to accompany text.

Think about getting ready for a school trip. Can they think what kinds of instructions teachers would give them? Look at the example of a list with the heading 'Things you will need', on page 31. Draw attention to the use of the colon. Also, comment upon how the adjectives have been used to describe the kinds of thing needed.

Pose the question: 'We often need instructions when we are going to do something for the first time, like going to the swimming baths. Can you write a new list about what you will need if you are going to the swimming baths?' (two minutes) Return to the class example of the school trip, and look at the way the instructions have been written. Just like the recipe they are numbered and each of the sentences has a verb at or near the beginning. There are also some diagrams to help.

Now ask them to think about some of the things that they will have to remember to do when they go to the swimming baths. They can use the planning sheet to write down their instructions. Remind them of how to use verbs and to think about any diagrams they may want to use which might help the reader. Important note: not everything may need a picture.

Children can use the plenary to share their instructions with a partner. The partners can then comment on how successful the instructions have been:

▲ can they understand the instructions?
▲ are they clearly written?
▲ have they chosen the best verbs?
▲ what do they like about the instructions?
▲ what could be improved and how?

Follow up Work
A combination of the class instructions could then be used for a poster to remind children about what to do on a swimming day. This could also be produced in leaflet form to help younger children when they first go to the baths, or for future classes.

Resources
My first cook book – Angela Wilkes – Dorling Kindersley.
Winnie the Pooh cook book – WHSmith

Key pointers when choosing a book:

▲ simple easy to follow recipes
▲ clear step by step photographs/illustrations
▲ clear labelling
▲ appropriate captions
▲ language suitable for age of reader
▲ index and contents page

Getting ready for a school trip

Things you will need:

A warm coat
A small bag
£2 spending money
some flat shoes
a packed lunch

1. Bring your lunch in a small bag which can be carried easily. Don't bring any glass bottles.

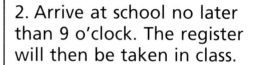

2. Arrive at school no later than 9 o'clock. The register will then be taken in class.

3. Make sure that you have any money or valuables in a safe place before you leave.

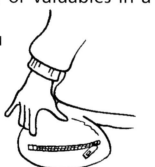

4. Tell your teacher if you get travel sick. Ask your teacher to look after any travel sickness pills you need to take.

5. Wait with a partner for the coach to arrive. When it stops do not rush to get on. Wait for your teacher to tell you where to sit.

6. Stay in your seat while the coach is moving.

Going to the swimming baths

5
Persuasion

Lesson Plan

Whole Class Work – Text Study

Read a set of sentences to children that are a combination of fact and opinion (see page 35 for examples). Ask the children in groups of four to brainstorm the differences. Encourage the children to explain which words or phrases helped them to reach their decision. Explain that fact is what we know and that opinion is what we think we know.

Group/Class Activity

Present the children with an advertising feature on their local area and a far-away place they have been studying in geography (for examples see pages 36 and 37). Ask them to read the feature according to a set of instructions:

1. Choose two colours. Underline the words and phrases that you think are fact in one colour and those that you think are opinions in the other colour.
2. List the things in the advertisement that you would like to do and the things you would not.
3. Discuss in pairs who the advert might be written for – who would read it?
4. Choose one word or phrase that makes you feel the advert is not accurate.

Stop the children at various points during the activity to reinforce what we understand by fact and opinion. They should work in pairs within their groups and discuss each set of instructions.

Plenary

Ask the children to share some of the factual and opinion words that they have highlighted. Reinforce the point that certain words are used to change the context of a text.

Follow-up Activity

Children can write a letter to the travel agency pointing out why the information on the area is not accurate and arguing that it should not be published.

Fact Or Opinion?

	Fact	Opinion
1. Kenya is in East Africa.		
2. I think that's a brilliant idea!		
3. Acorns grow on oak trees.		
4. Strawberry is the best flavour for ice cream.		
5. Great Bridge is an interesting place to visit.		
6. You should always put on a coat when you go out.		
7. Karen is a beautiful name.		
8. Dogs make better pets than cats.		

Great Bridge

Spend a fun-filled day in Great Bridge.

Great Bridge lies in the heart of the Black Country with easy access to the busy centres of Birmingham, Walsall and Wolverhampton.

Whether you are eight or eighty there is always so much to do. A regular bus service will take the children to the adventure hideout 'Go Kidz Go' – where all their dreams are guaranteed to come true!

Why not enjoy a delicious meal at MacDonalds, where mouthwatering burgers are served? Afterwards stroll towards the canal side where you can enjoy the peaceful surroundings or take a barge down the canal. Birds from many lands come to rest on the canal. The sound of their singing is like music to the ears! The flocks of ducks and swans around the canalside create an idyllic nature reserve not be missed.

Kenya

Enjoy a holiday of a lifetime amongst the most spectacular wildlife in the world.

Kenya, in the heart of East Africa, is most famous for not only its National Parks but also the peaceful white coral shores that stretch for miles. It is a place where the sun always shines and the rain rarely falls, and the beaches are always full of happy, smiling children.

Of all the experiences that a holiday can bring and all the memories it can provide, there is nothing as spectacular as the first sight of animals in the wild.

A safari is an exciting journey, leaving cities and towns far behind and going to a place full of wild animals living proud and free in their natural habitat. Keep your eyes peeled for the Big Five: rhino, elephant, lion, leopard and buffalo. You can also expect to see zebra, giraffe and monkeys – you'll tingle with fear just at the sight of it.

An excellent choice for all the family. Imagine the soft powder beaches where you can either relax in the sunshine or enjoy a range of water sports. There is no other holiday in the world that will provide you with this variety and excitement. So, whatever your pleasure, we promise to satisfy your every wish.

6
Factual writing

Lesson Plan

Whole Class Work – Text Study

Using pictures of Greek gods/goddesses (we used a Folens' picture resource pack) children produce a piece of factual writing focusing upon the process of writing and the various stages involved.

Children work in groups and are assigned roles and responsibilities. Each group has a picture and has ten minutes to brainstorm around the picture. Model the process by describing what can be seen, what feelings it arouses, personal responses and what it would be like to be in the picture. After ten minutes children pass their picture to another group who have to read what has been written and then add their own ideas. Emphasize that this is the planning stage and that children should not be pointing out spelling mistakes or criticising work. Demonstrate ways in which they may add to the brainstorm, focusing on key features of pictures and the use of adjectives to describe them.

Group/Class Activities

Return the pictures to the original groups and ask them to read the descriptions. As a group they can select ideas that they feel would be most useful to explain or describe. A writing frame is then used to structure the children's writing before they edit/revise the finished product for sharing with others. Explain the writing frame to the children and brainstorm key words to help them (see page 40 for an example).

Encourage children to be editors in the sense that they may decide not to use pieces which they do not feel would fit in well with their writing. In their groups children can think about and highlight key ideas on the planning sheet that they will want to include in their writing. Show the children how to use envoy techniques* to share their ideas with other groups and to justify why certain ideas were omitted from their planning sheet.

Plenary
Children highlight ways in which they have worked which have helped them to think of a variety of ideas for their writing. Children offer examples of ways in which they have used language creatively to describe the picture.

Follow Up Work
Children can present their writing to the rest of the class and focus upon the skills of presentation.

*Envoy technique involves sending a messenger from one group to another, to share ideas

Ancient Greece

This picture shows

When I look at this picture I feel

If I was a character in the picture I think I would

I am interested in finding out more about

Key words:

7
Sequencing text

Lesson Plan

Whole Class Work – Text Study
Shared read of Perseus the Gorgon-Slayer. Tell the children that the myth they have been looking at is an example of a quest. Explain to the children why: Perseus goes on a quest and along the way he is given objects and overcomes obstacles before he achieves his final goal and returns to the point from which he started. Explain to the children that the story is organised into sections – can the children remember any of these? Record their answers on the board. Explain that it is an episodic story – each event leads to the next.

Group/Class Activities
Ask the children, in pairs, to use a writing frame to help them sequence the order of the obstacles that Perseus was faced with and what objects he used. Explain to the children that they are using the writing frame to help them organise a retelling of the story. Tell the children that they will need to only write in notes. (An example writing frame is shown on page 44.)

Plenary
Children can explain what Perseus was trying to get, and what his final goal was, before he achieved his aim.

Follow Up Work
In pairs, children can draw one picture from each episode/ section of the story. Give children a starting point and explain that they are to record the most important parts in the story. After they have represented the story they can write a caption to each section indicating the main action. Children can then collaboratively write a sequel.

Writing a sequel

Previous learning:
Children should be aware of the structure and features of the story form for a quest.

Key learning focus:
Collaboratively, children will write a sequel to the Perseus story, in the style of a quest.

Children will write with a particular audience in mind.

Assessment opportunities:
Do children understand the structure of a quest?

Main Activity:
Recap on previous work using the story of Perseus.

Children can tell their partners what they understand by the word quest.

Brainstorm and scribe key features of a quest on the board or flip chart.

Explain to the children that the key focus for the session is to write a sequel for parents and as part of a presentation to Year 6 children.

Explain to children that they will be working collaboratively in fours, and as a group they need to decide appropriate roles and responsibilities.

As a class, shared write the opening and closing of the sequel using the planning framework.

Give the children step-by-step instructions on completing the planning framework.

In twos within their groups, each pair then has to think of two problems faced by Perseus in his new quest. Pairs swap the problems and then have the task of solving each other's problem by finding a solution which involves an object. The object can be used as a tool to help solve the problem. Children have five minutes for each task and then as a group they record their problems/solutions.

This is followed by whole class discussion.

Direct teach that each problem/solution in a quest can be seen as an episode. Each episode should have one main event which is self-contained and therefore will easily fit with other episodes.

Children now individually take one episode and write four or five sentences with illustration as to what happens. They have ten minutes.

As a group the four episodes are sequenced in terms of the best order. Children have to think whether their episodes need to be connected using certain link words. Children then become editors and revise their sequel as a group, bearing in mind that one audience they are writing for is their parents.

Plenary
One group shares their sequel while the rest of the class listens and decides whether it is written in the style of a quest.

Perseus' quest

What did Perseus have to get?

What gets in the way and makes it difficult for Perseus?

What does Perseus have to collect to help him?

How does the quest end?

8
Using artefacts

Lesson Plan

Whole Class Work – Text Study
Children work to produce a data card for each artefact with information for both teachers and children.

Guide the children through three sets of questions to help investigate their object for the data cards. These focus upon the physical features of the object, the purpose of the object and its usage. (For examples of questions cards, see pages 47 to 49.)

Group/Class Activities
Children work in groups and focus upon the different questions to help structure their data card. Model how to record their answers. Within the group, one role would be to draw the object accurately. Children can decide within their groups how they will find the answers to the questions and what they will need to help them. Appropriate books should be made accessible to children, but do make sure you have checked that they contain relevant information for the tasks. Once the children have worked on the separate elements of the research they need to organise the relevant and important information for their data card. Demonstrate that only three important things should be on the data card as too much information will not be useful. Discuss what people will need to know about the object.

Plenary
Children could present their object through a slide show, where the data card provides them with the commentary. Their commentary could be tape recorded so that they will be able

to analyse whether they have given enough information about the object. Another class or teachers could be the audience.

Follow Up Work
Children can turn their classroom into a museum and display objects with the data cards by them. Another class could be invited to walk through the exhibition and the children can talk them through the various artefacts they have been studying.

Artefacts used for this example were taken from the 'Buried treasures – Egypt' series available from WHSmith.

Using artefacts – questions list 1

What is it made of?

What colour is it?

Does it have a smell?

What does it sound like?

Are there signs of wear?

Is it hand-made?

Using artefacts – questions list 2

Why was it made?

How was it made?

Why is it valued?

Why is it interesting?

Using artefacts – questions list 3

When was it made?

How old is it?

Do we still have objects like it?

Who made it?

Who used it?

What is it worth to:
– the people who made it?
– the people who used it?
– the people who kept it?
– you?
– the bank?
– a museum?

9
Letter writing

Lesson Plan

Whole Class Work – Text Study

Working in groups of four, give each group a selection of letters labelled from A – F (see pages 53 to 59).

Explain to the children that you want them to look at the samples of writing that they have in front of them. Can they work out what kind of writing we are going to focus upon for the lesson? Give them one minute to scan the writing.

Ask the question: 'Why did you think they were all letters?' What were the main features that they identified? Explain that we are not looking at the writing itself but about how the letter has been set out – the structure. Ask the children to work in groups, reminding them of their targets – everyone should have a go at writing, and should listen carefully to each other's point of view. Explain that they have 7 coloured pencils as there are 7 different features of letter writing. Model how to use coloured pencils by circling each feature found in each letter. Ask the children to carry on scanning the letters in their groups. Brainstorm features as a class and record on a flip chart.

Group/Class Activities

Consider why we write letters. What purpose does letter-writing serve? Explain that we are going to look at the letters again and try to work out why they have been written. This time we will be looking at the content of the letters. To do this we will need to scan the writing but also skim to find some words which may help us. Model how to approach one of the letters: share the reading of one of the letters and talk through how to approach the text. Give the children four minutes to have a go at the other letters. Brainstorm as a class and list the purposes on a flip chart.

Explain that we are going to write a letter to send to another school. Explain the purpose behind it, and that the children need to consider the content of their letter.

Give each group a planning sheet for the whole group to record on. Put a sample letter for guided reading on the OHP. Read the whole letter, stating that its purpose is similar to the letter we are about to write, and that we can explore it to get some ideas for our own letter.

Read the opening, middle and end paragraphs. After each discuss the content of each one and get the children to work with a partner and note some ideas for each paragraph of their own letters inside the boxes on the planning sheet. (A sample planning sheet is shown on page 52.)

Return to the list of features written as a whole class earlier, to remind the children what they have to include for their writing to be a letter. Ask them to work in groups of four to produce a first draft letter, making sure that you support the less able. Ideas for the content should now be drawn from the children's planning sheets. Remind them of the targets set – that everyone should have a go; that they should listen to others' points of view; and what should be included. You could also set a time target for this of 15 minutes.

Plenary
Read aloud some of their letters.

Follow Up Work
Recap with the children why letters are written and who we could write to.

Explain to the children that letters are a means of saying something to someone who is not there – a means of communication. Encourage them to think about why they have a conversation. Letters are written to people you haven't seen, and tell you more than a day-to-day conversation.

Read the story, *Wish you were here* by Martina Selway. Explain to the children the context of the story is a set of letters. Read out Grandad's letter and explain to the children that Rosie has some problems. In pairs children can discuss what these could be.

Share and record responses on the board. Explain to children that they are going to take on the role of Rosie's Grandad and that they are going to write to Rosie with the solutions to her problems (so the children now have a purpose for writing a letter). In pairs children can think about the content of the letter, remembering from the previous session how to format it correctly.

Model this for the children on the board. Children can use their previous planning sheet to help them structure their letter.

Letter-writing planning sheet

A

7 Wessex Road,
West Bromwich,
West Midlands.
B35 7HN

24th April

Dear Sir,

Last week I moved into my new house in West Bromwich. I have unpacked all my boxes but cannot find my pension book.

Could you send me a new book as soon as possible. I have not got much money left and I need to pay my electricity bill. I am worried I will get cut off.

I hope to hear from you soon.

Yours sincerely,

B

16 Peters Close,
Wednesbury,
West Midlands.
B10 8BH

16th May

Dear Sam,

Thank you very much for my birthday present. It was a big surprise.

I had a really good day. I had a party at MacDonald's. It wasn't very funny when Mum lost the car keys. We all thought we would have to stay the night.

I took lots of photos of the party. Will send you one with this letter.

Best wishes,

P.S. Let me know what you think of my photo.

C

31 St George's Road,
Great Bridge,
West Midlands.
B6 6LY

12th June

Dear Madam,

Six weeks ago I sent you an order for a blue jumper. A parcel came today and it was a red one.

I am not very happy. I have had to wait a very long time. It is not the colour I wanted.

I am returning the jumper to you and want all my money back.

Yours sincerely,

D

22 Whitechurch Road,
Tipton,
West Midlands.
DY9 8RT

21st March

Dear Jane,

How are you? It has been a long time since I saw you.

I am sending you the book I promised. I won't be reading it because we are going on holiday. We are going away for two weeks.

I will ring you when I get back.

Best wishes,

E

6 Severn Close,
Dudley,
West Midlands.
DY11 3RX

29th September

Dear Sue,

We would like you to come to a disco at our club next week. It is being held to raise money for charity.

The doors open at 8 o'clock and the band begins at half past eight. Hot dogs will be on sale and there is a raffle too.

We do hope that you will be able to come.

Best wishes,

P.S. Bring a friend if you can

F

Wheeley Brook
Primary School,
Fenchurch Lane,
Penrith,
Cumbria.
CA8 4WP

12th February

Dear Class Five,

It will soon be time for us to come and see your school. We have been getting ready for our visit and have collected lots of things from the countryside to show you.

Our school is different from yours. We have lots of fields at the back. It is also very small so it will be interesting to visit somewhere in the middle of a busy city.

We will be arriving on the morning of Monday 7th March. This means we can spend the afternoon with you in your lessons. We are looking forward to seeing you soon.

Best wishes,